This Coloring Book
Belongs To

Color Palette

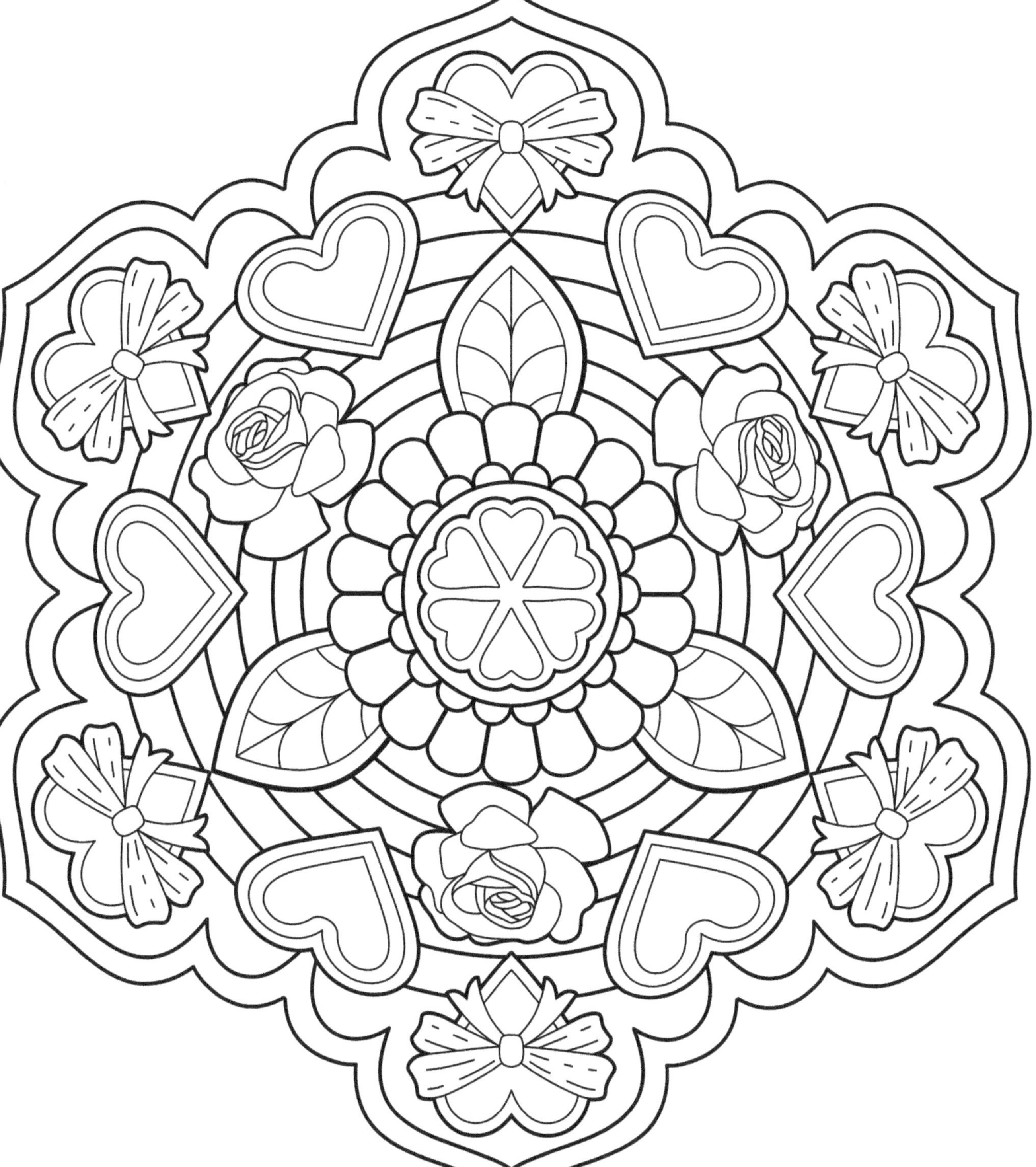

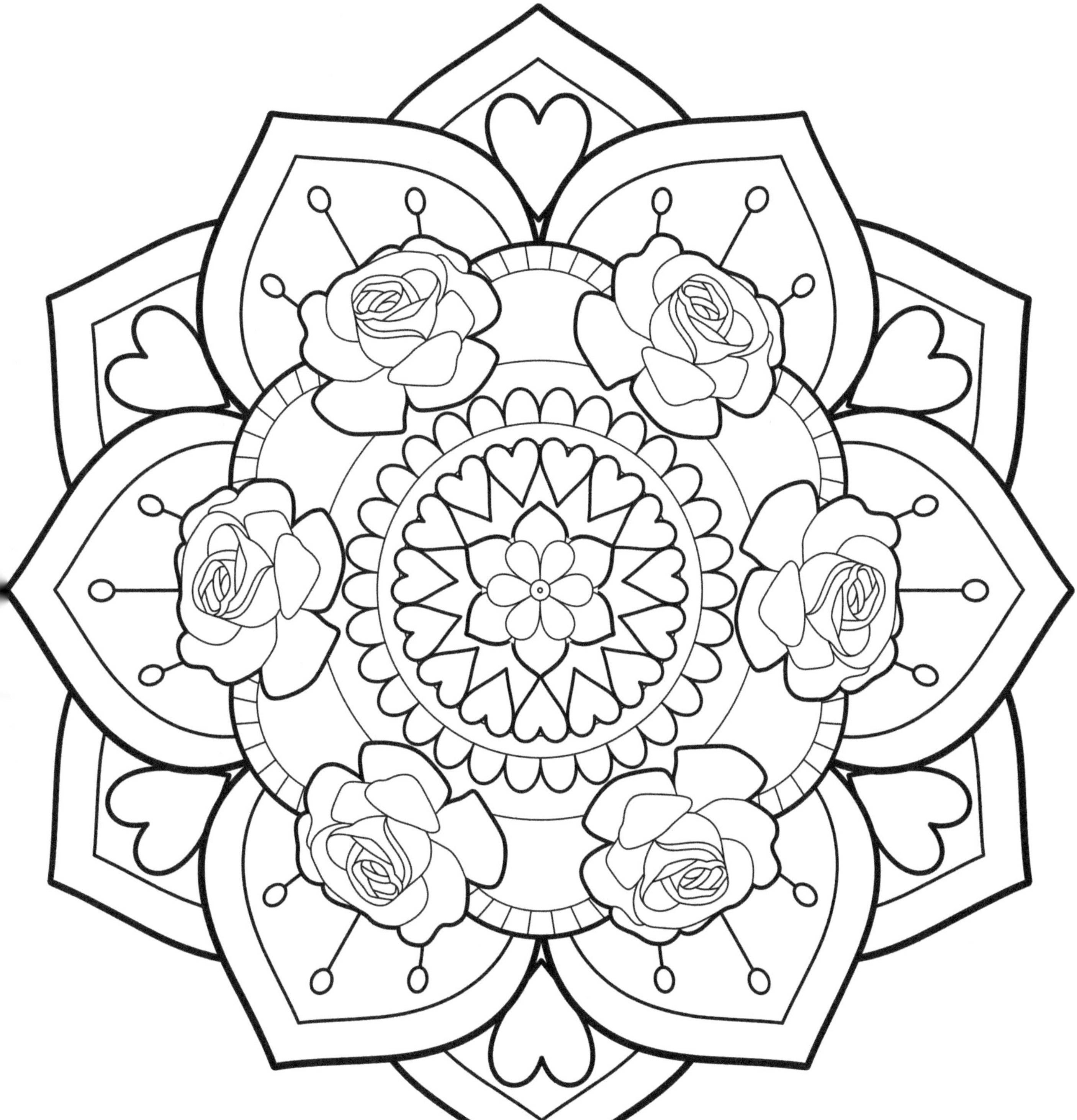

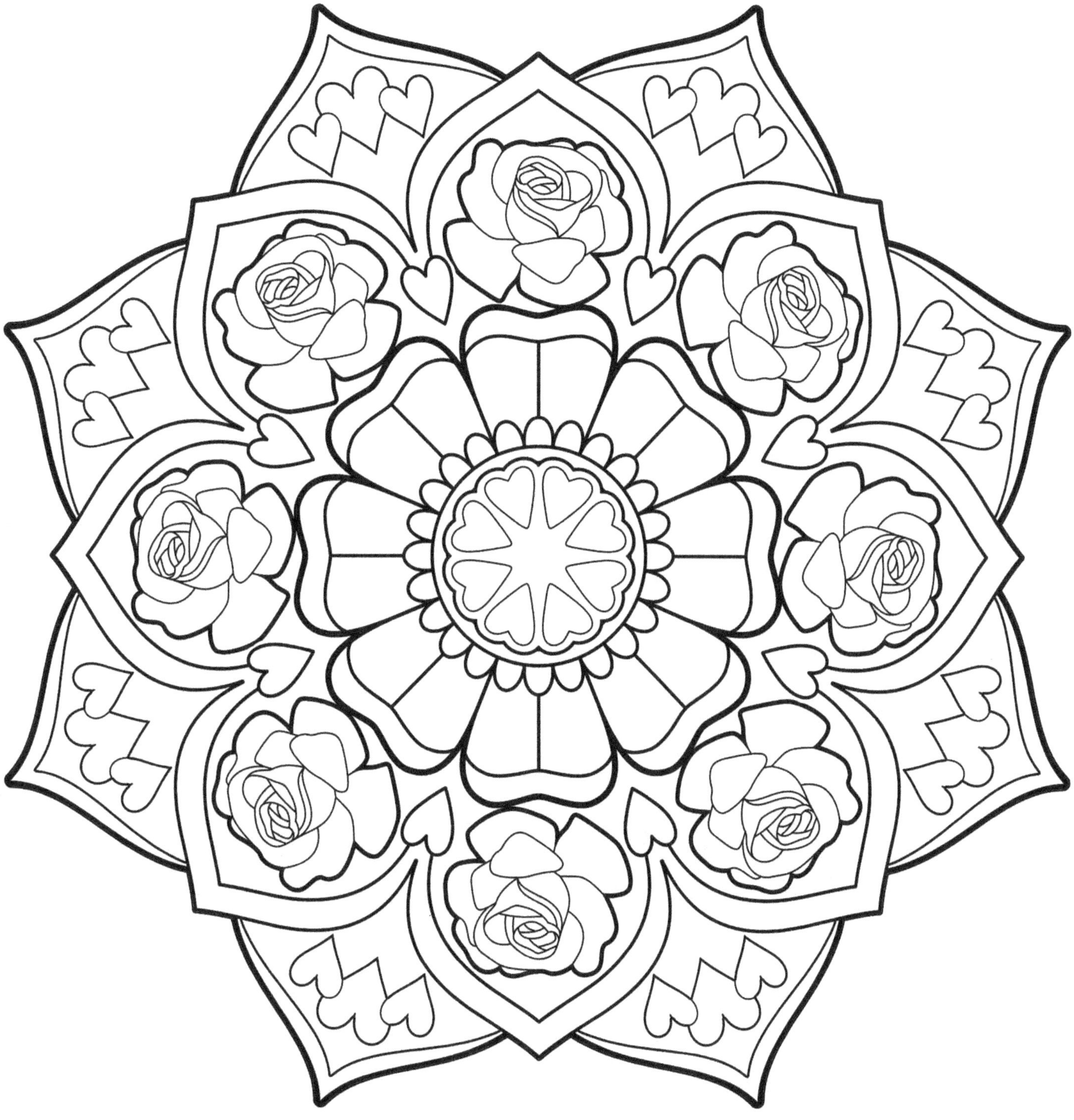

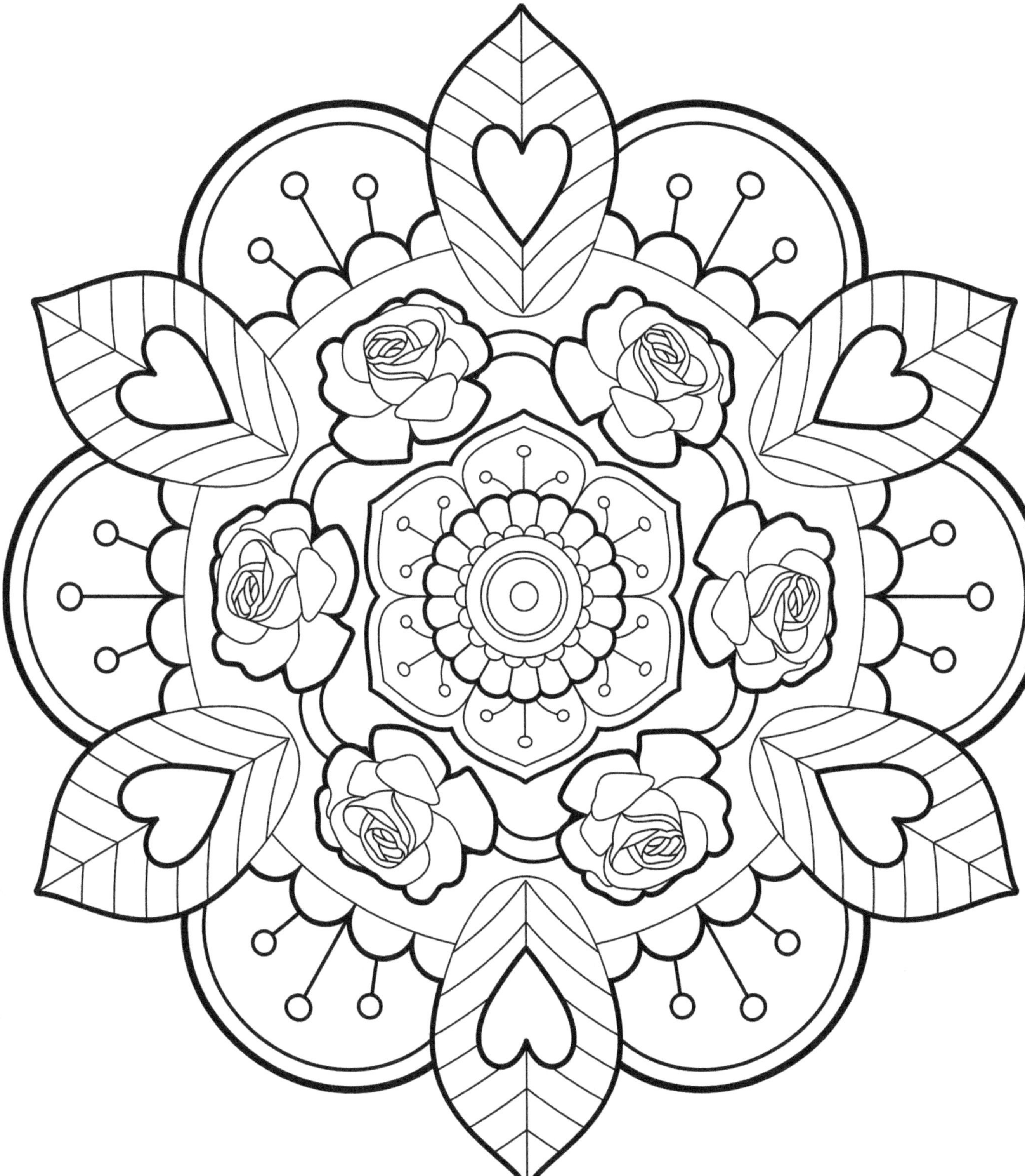

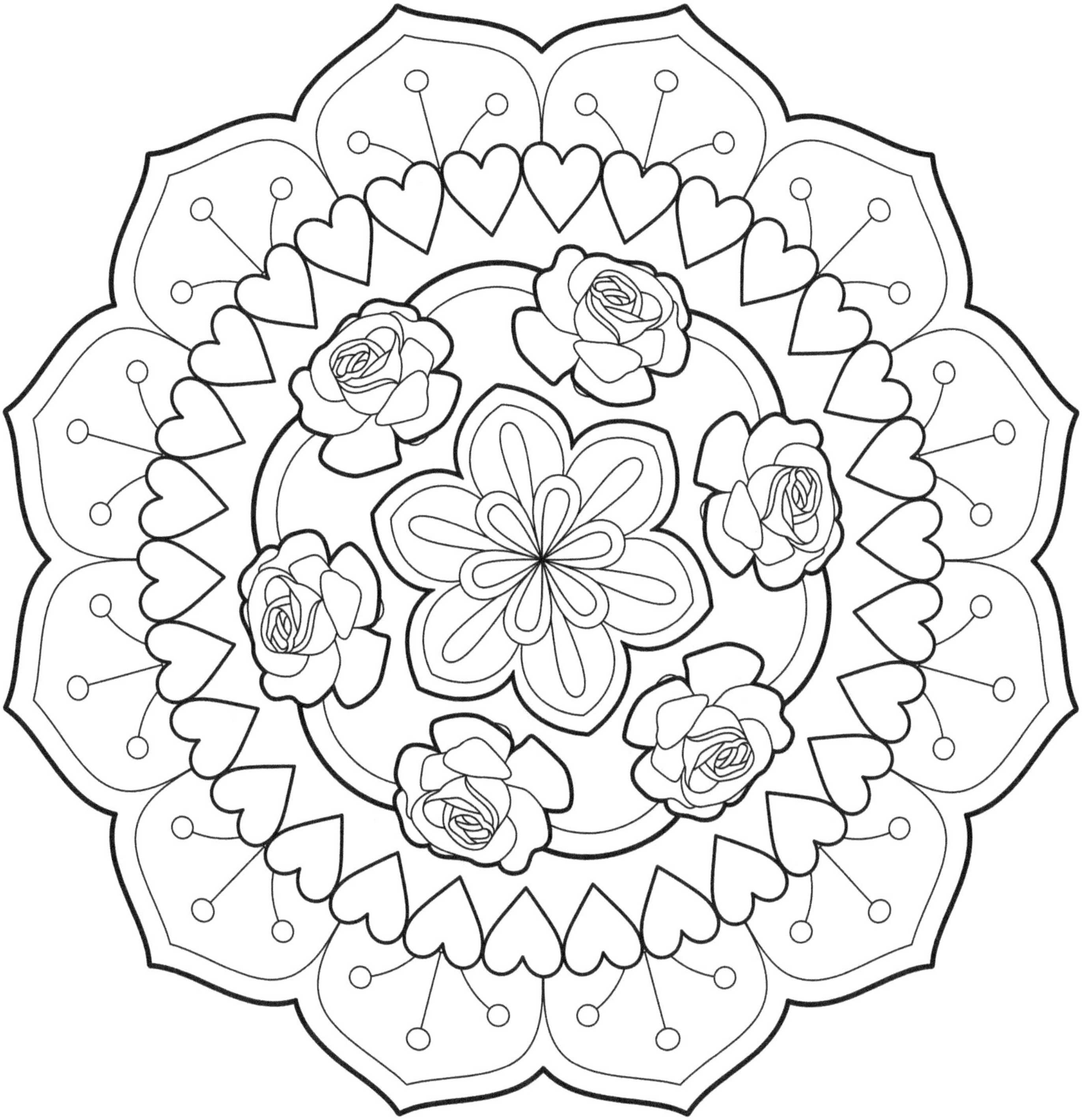

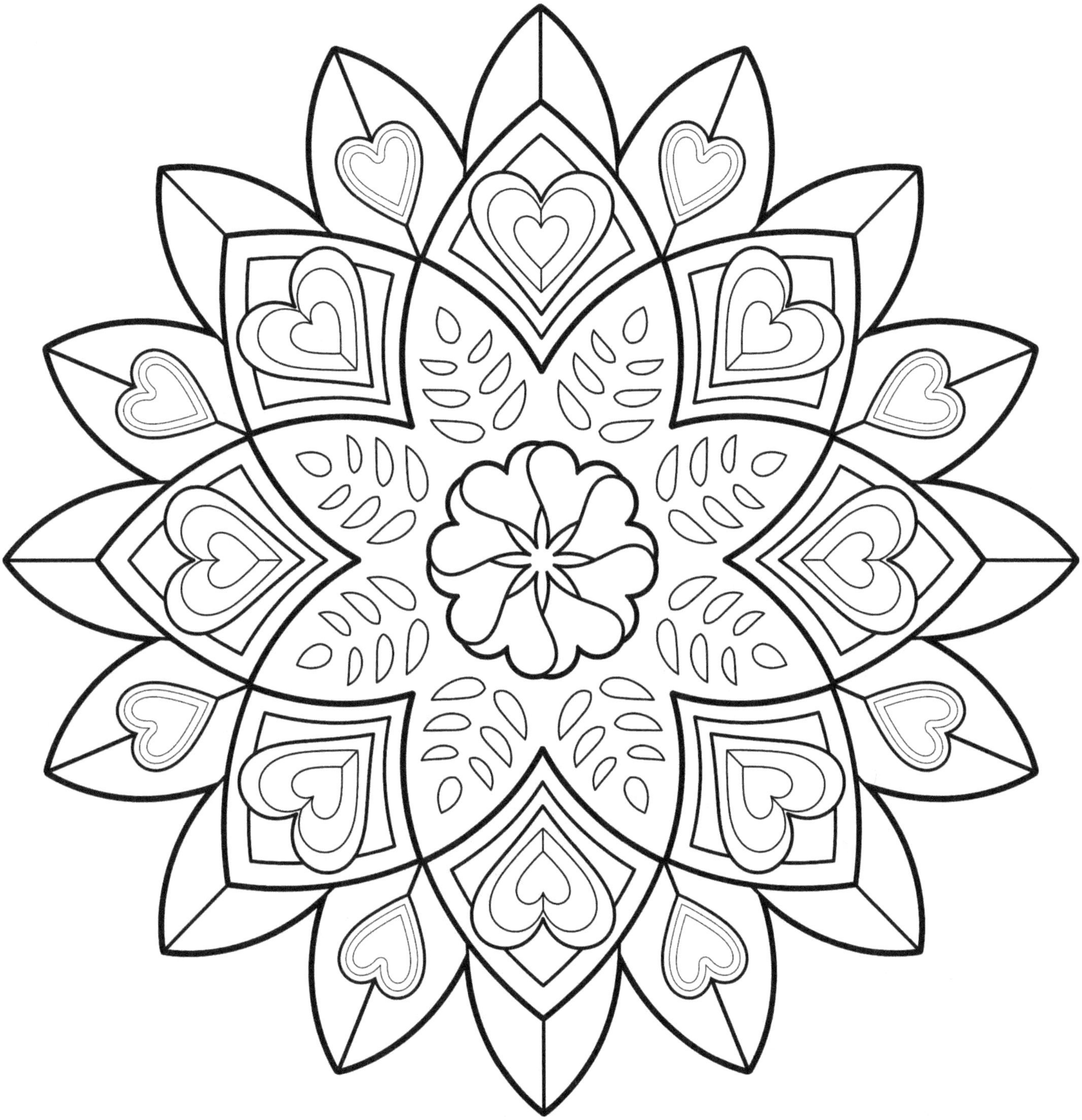

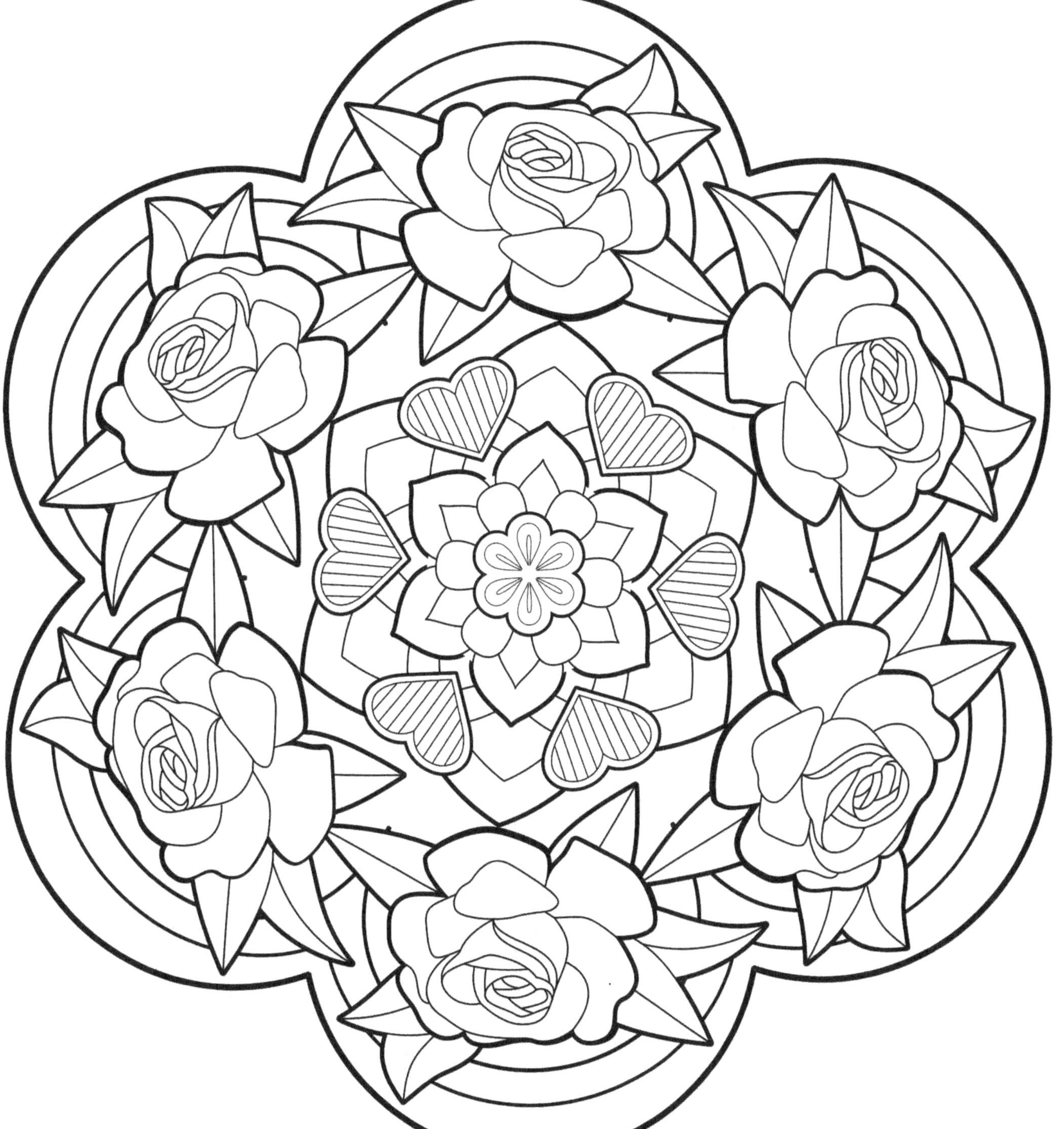

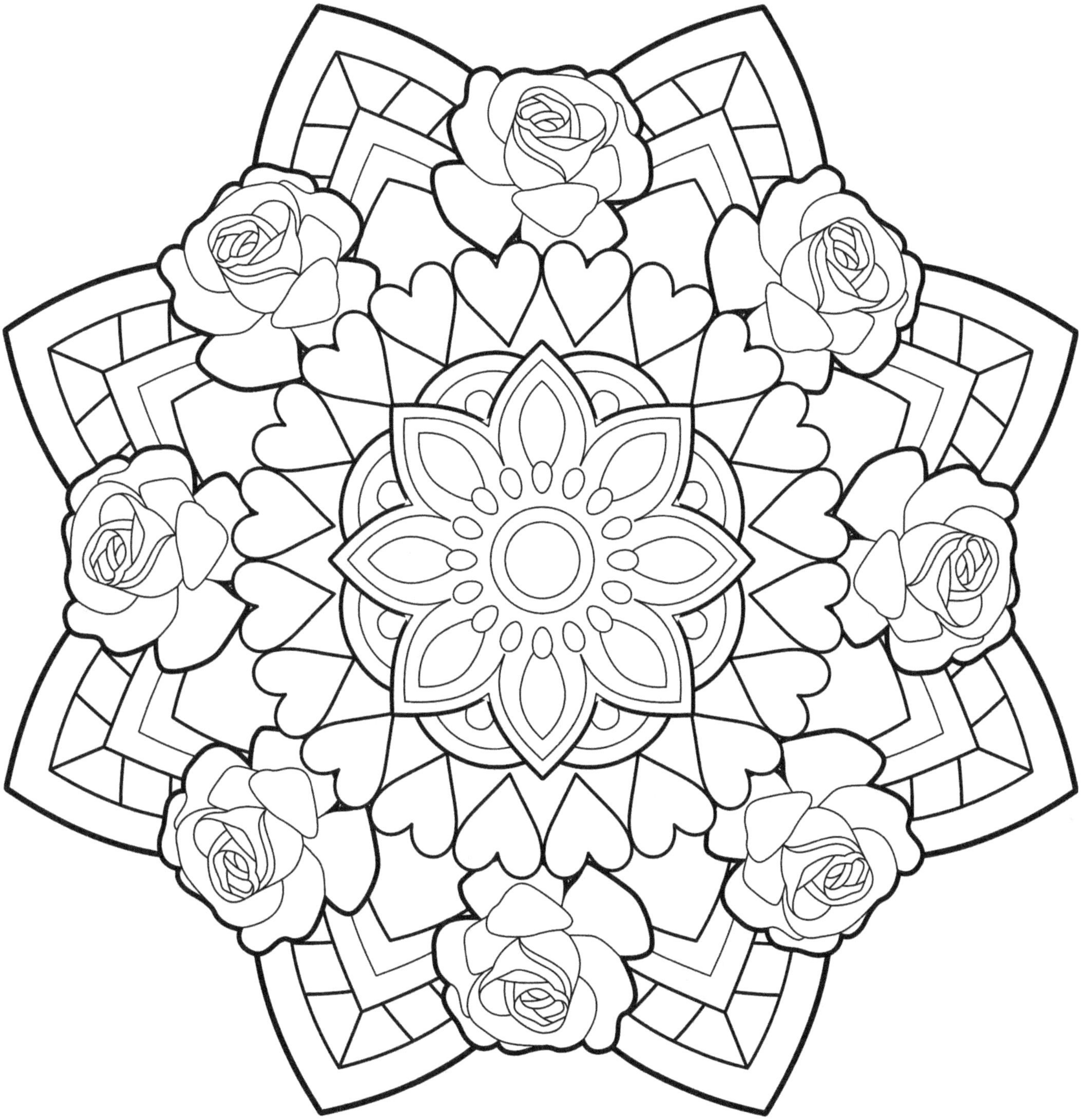

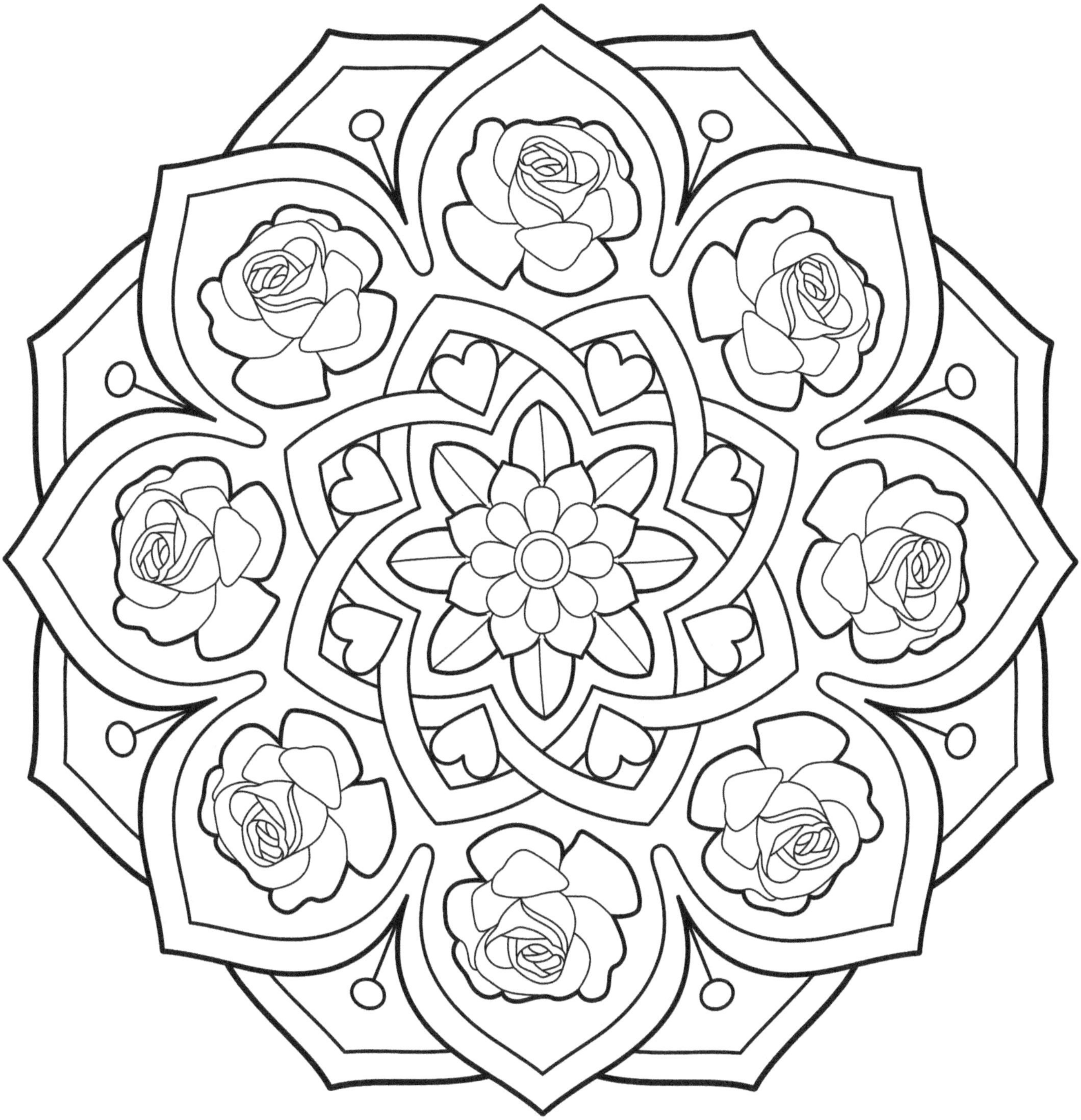

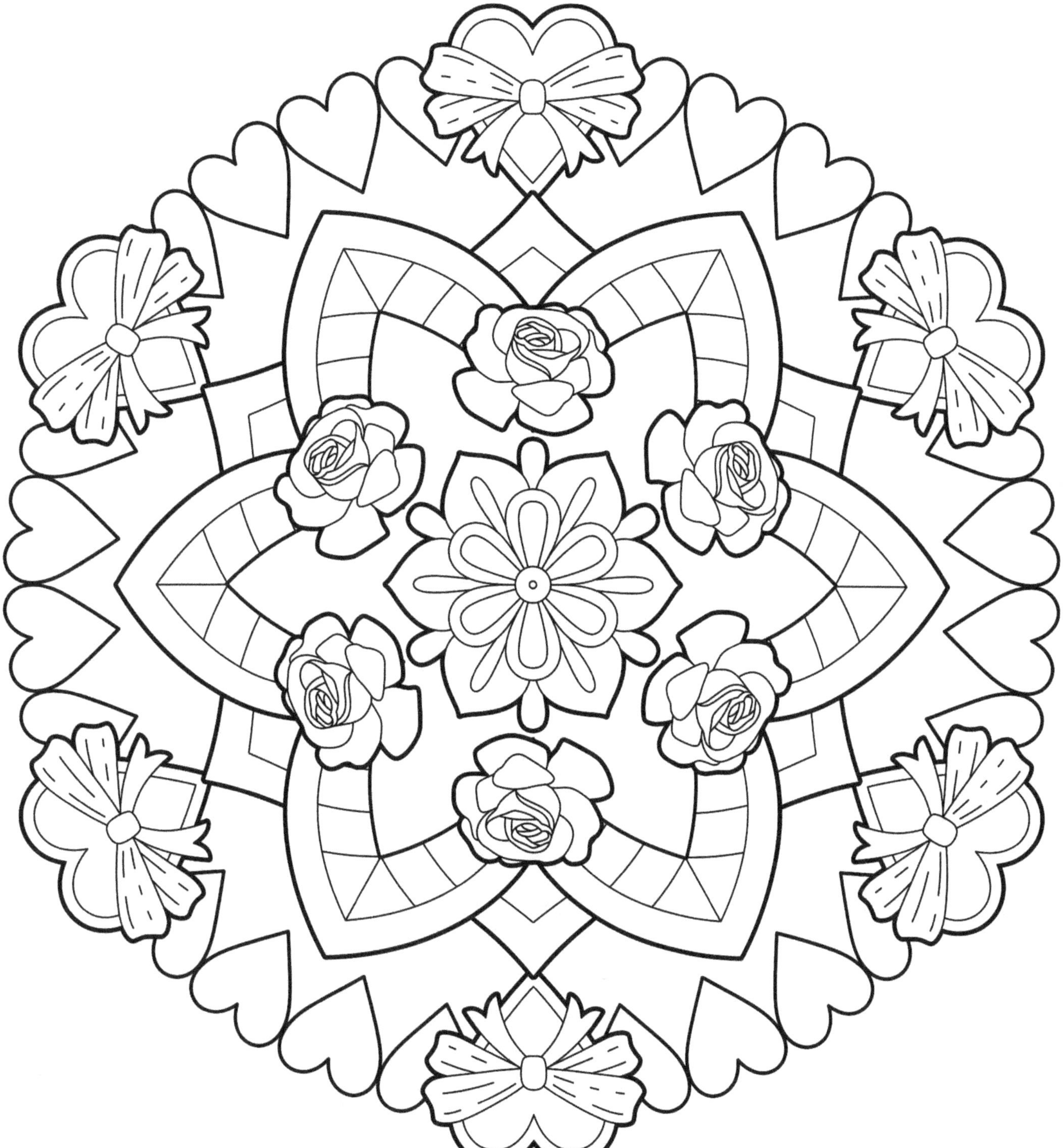

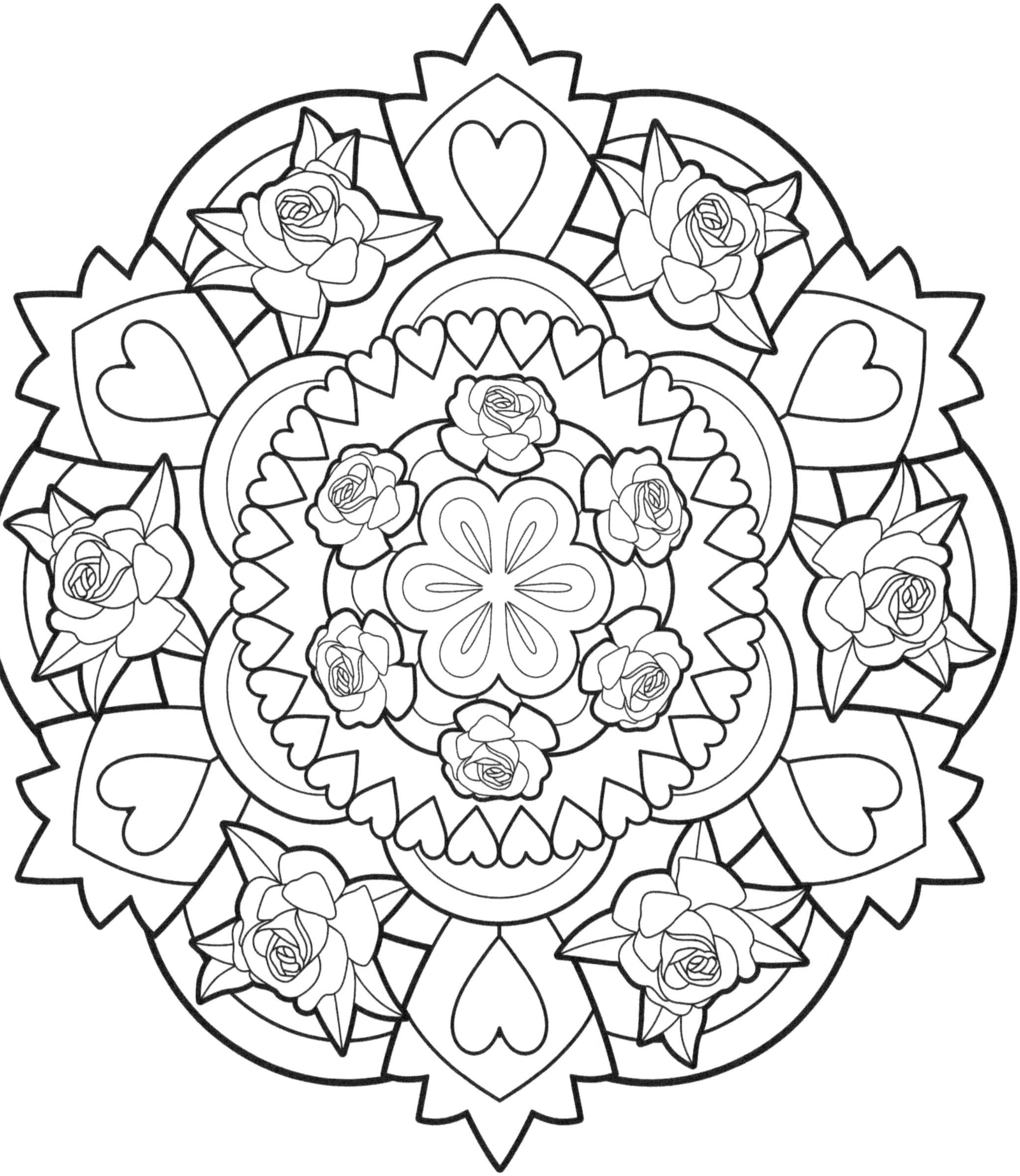

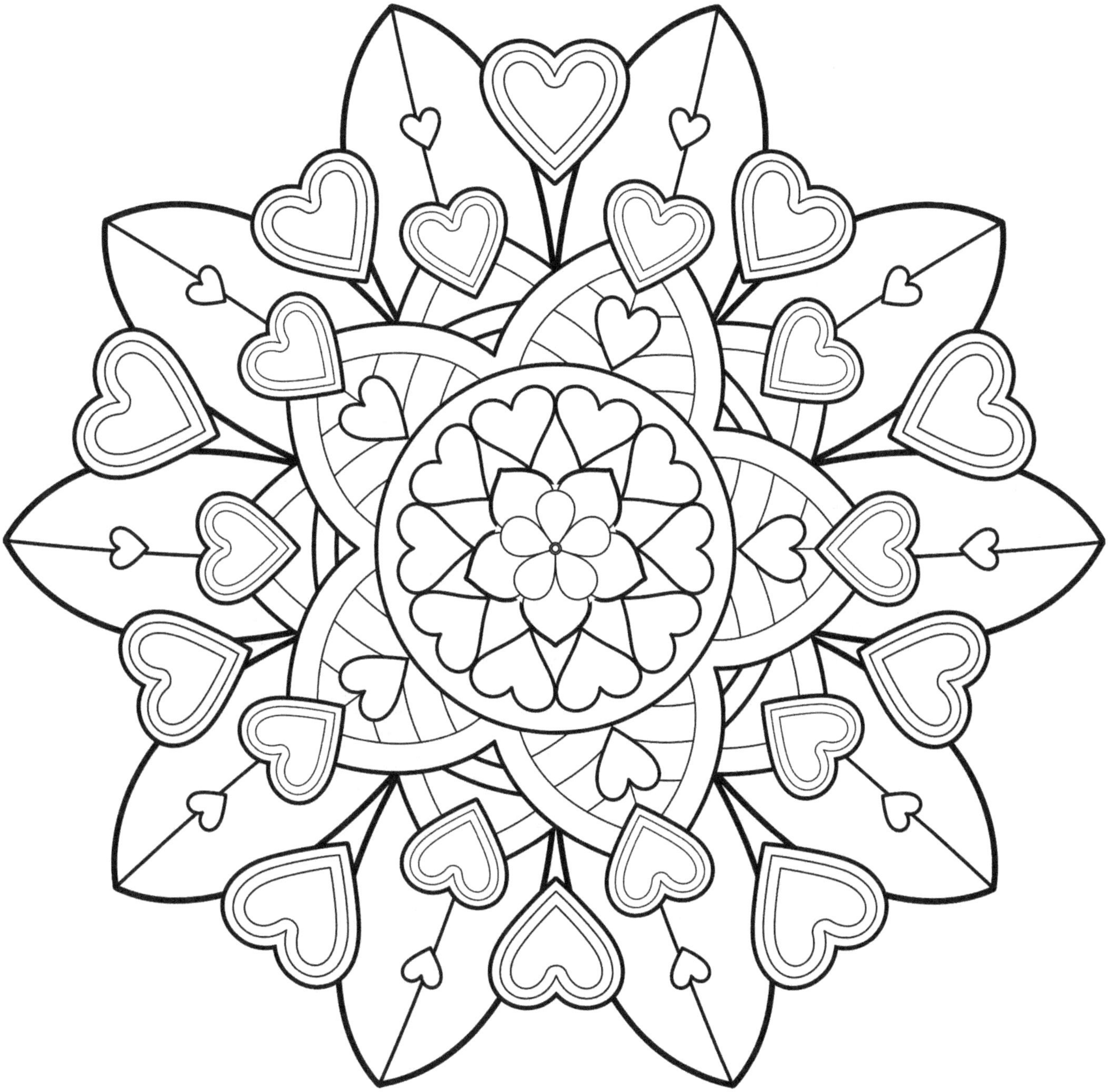

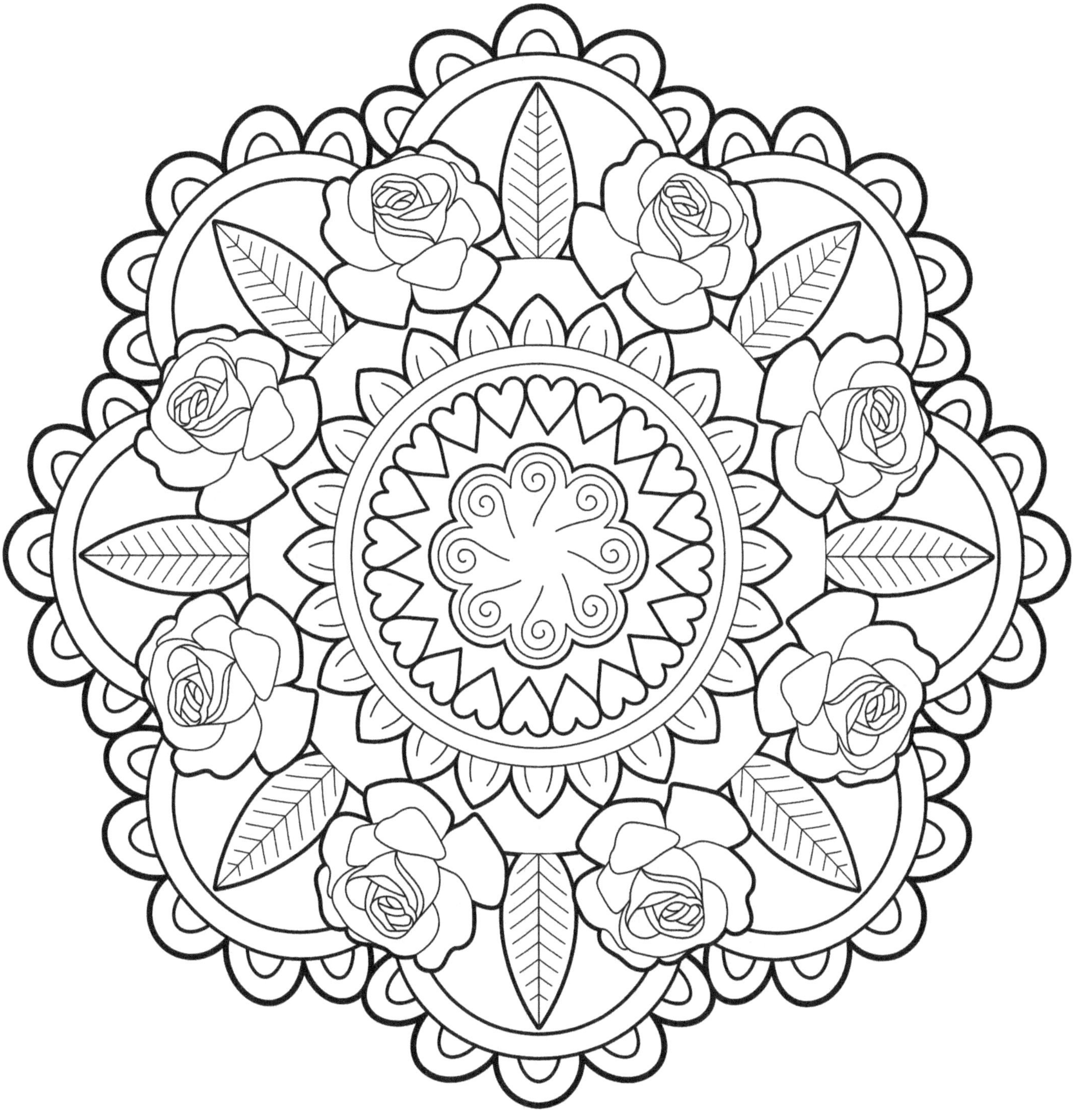

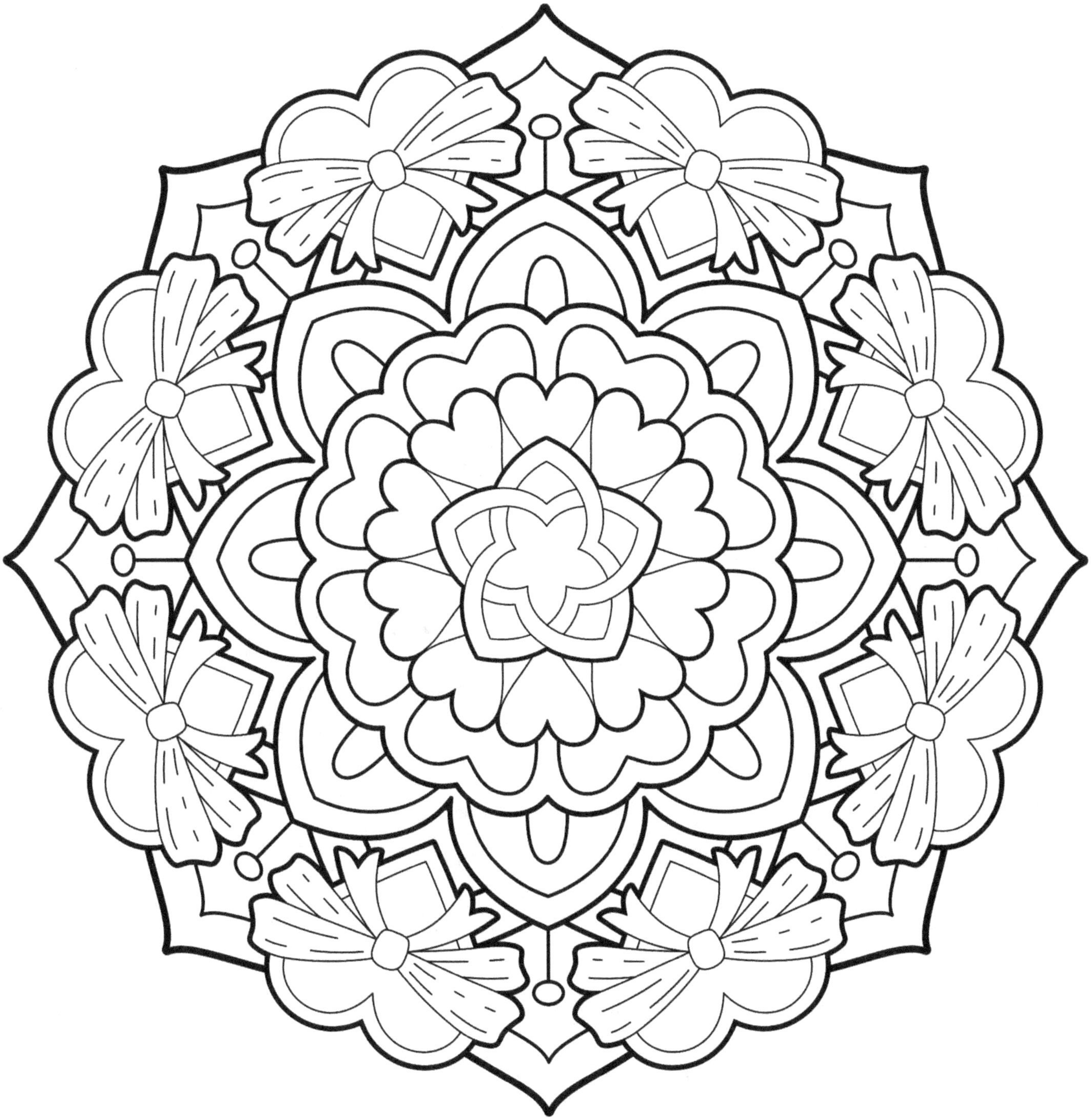

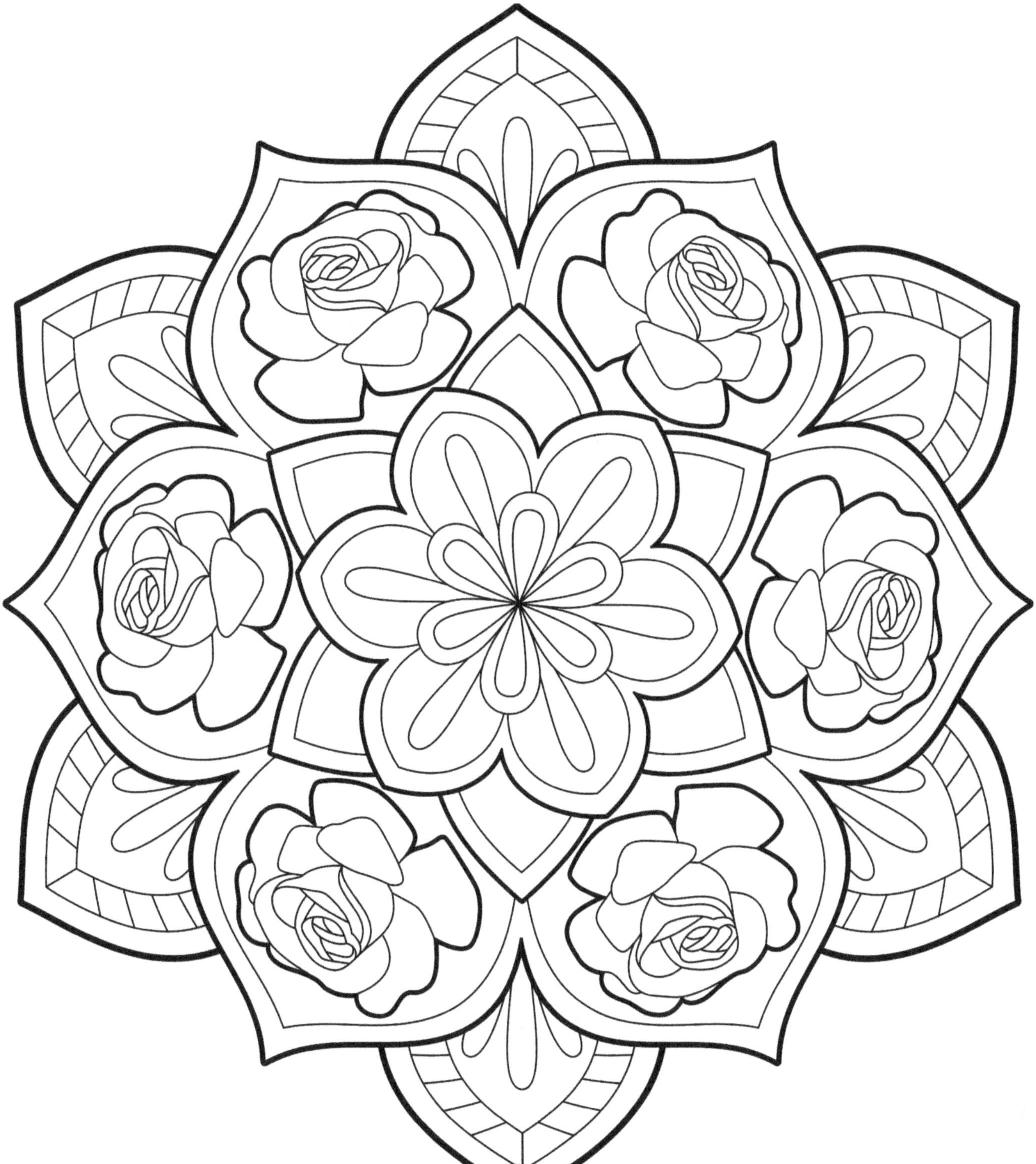

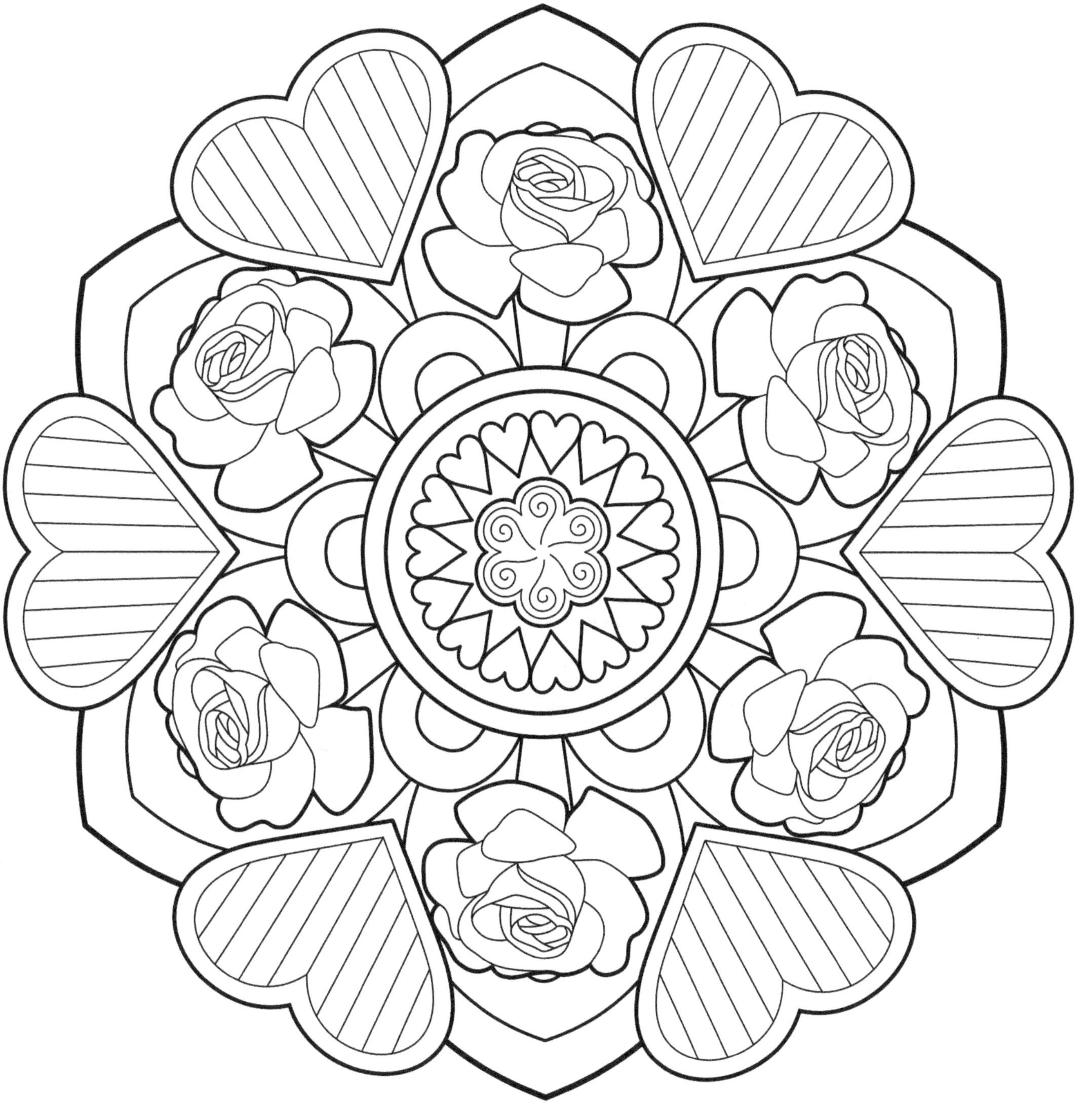

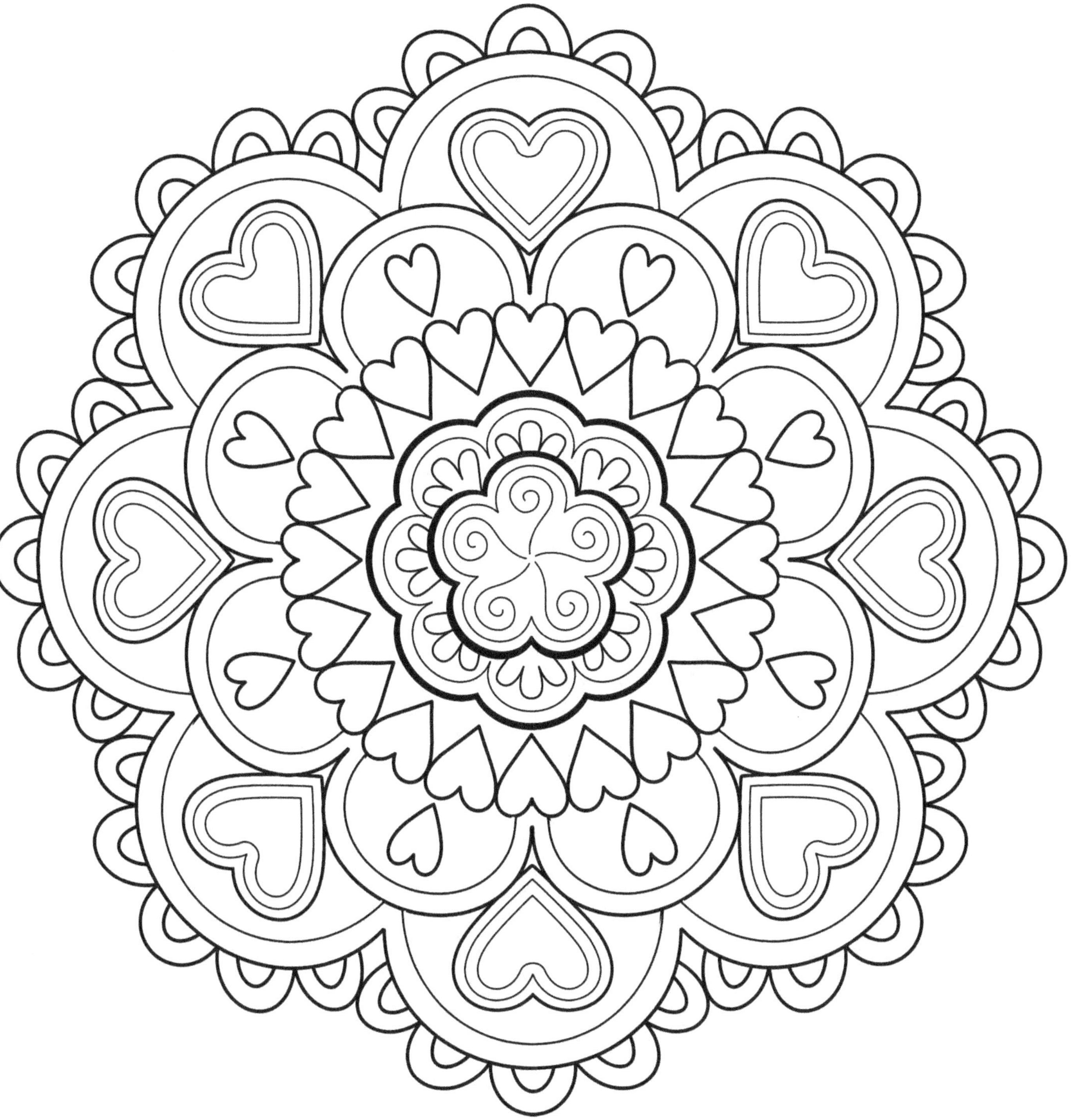

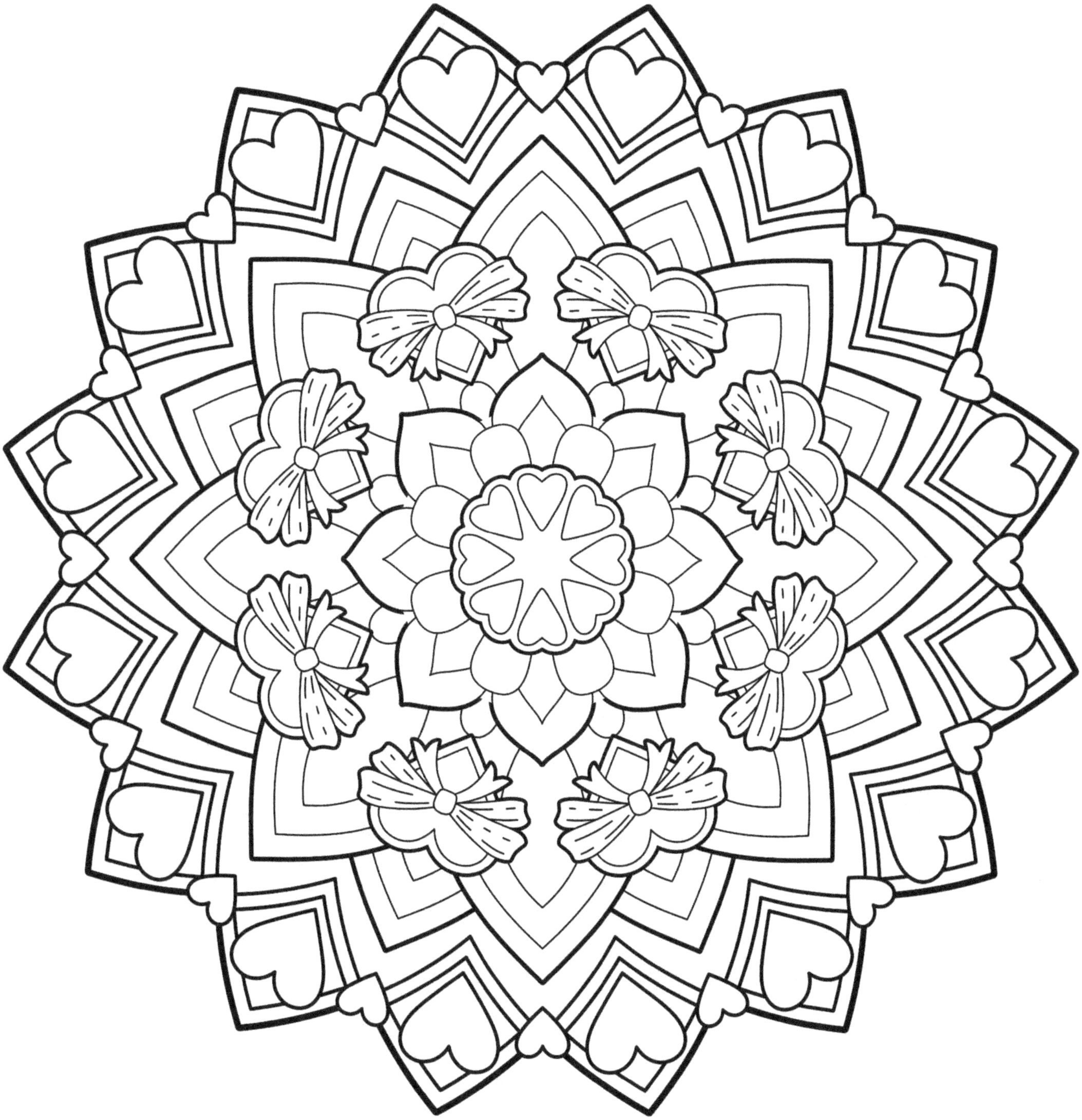

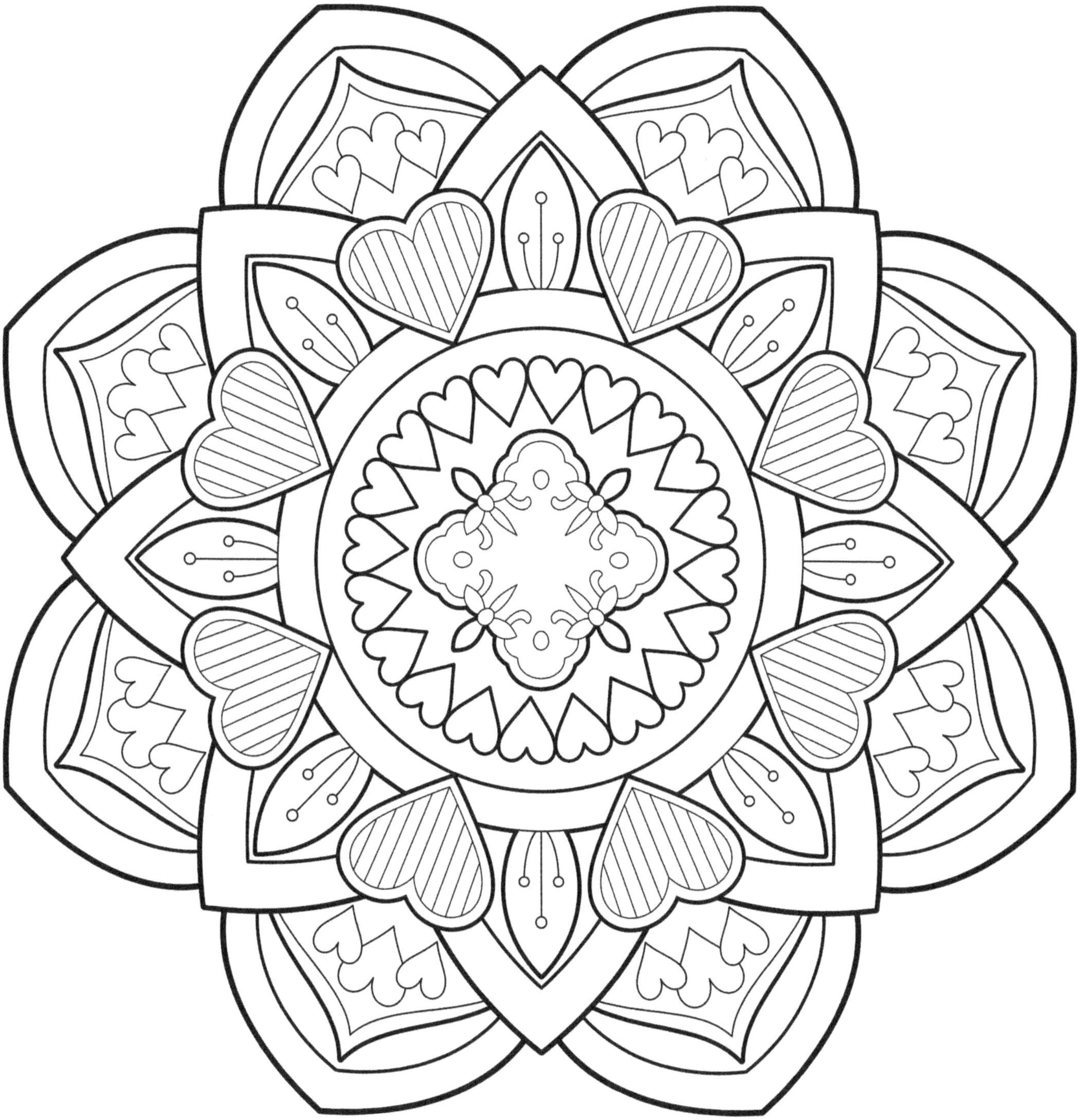

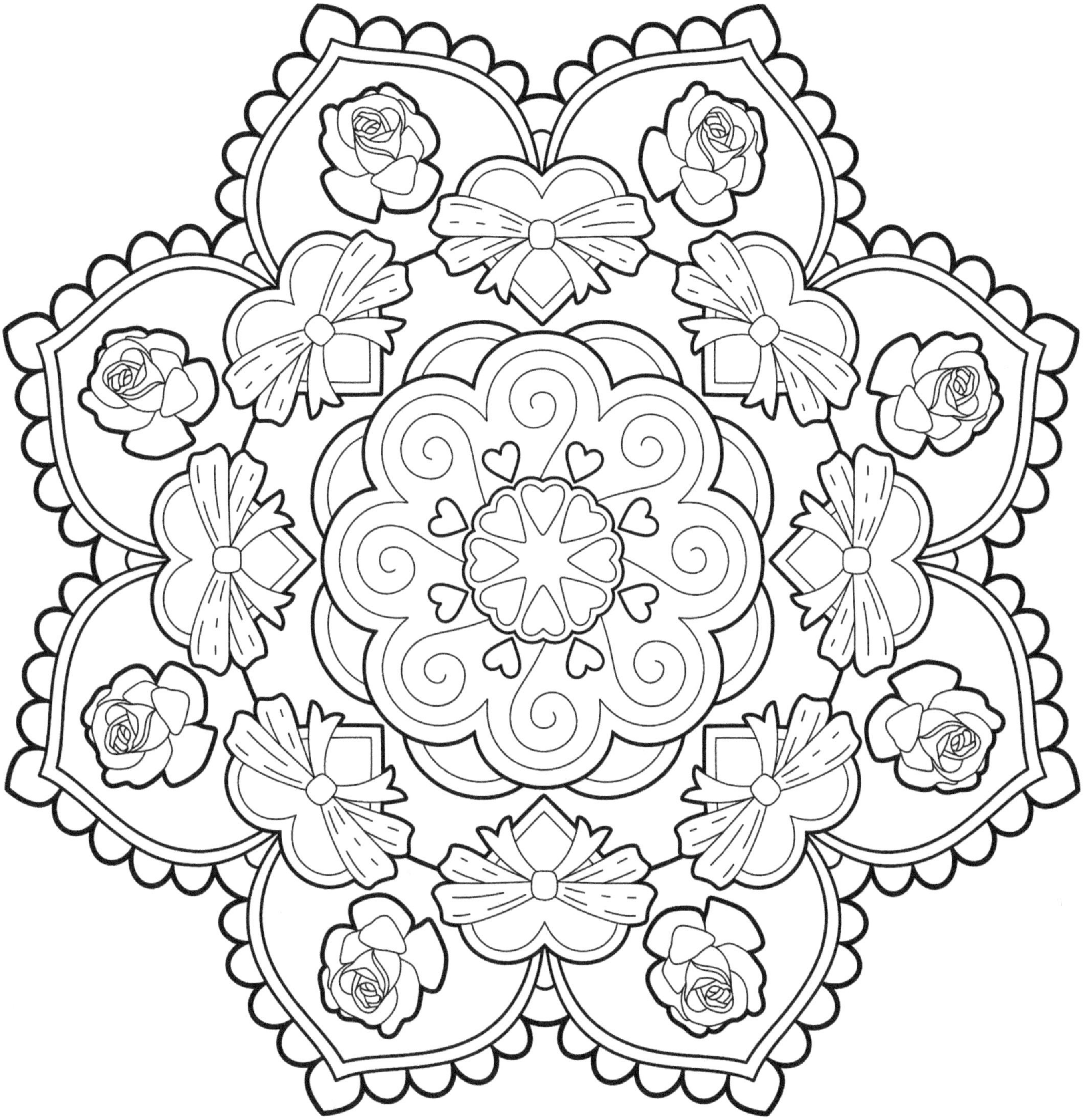

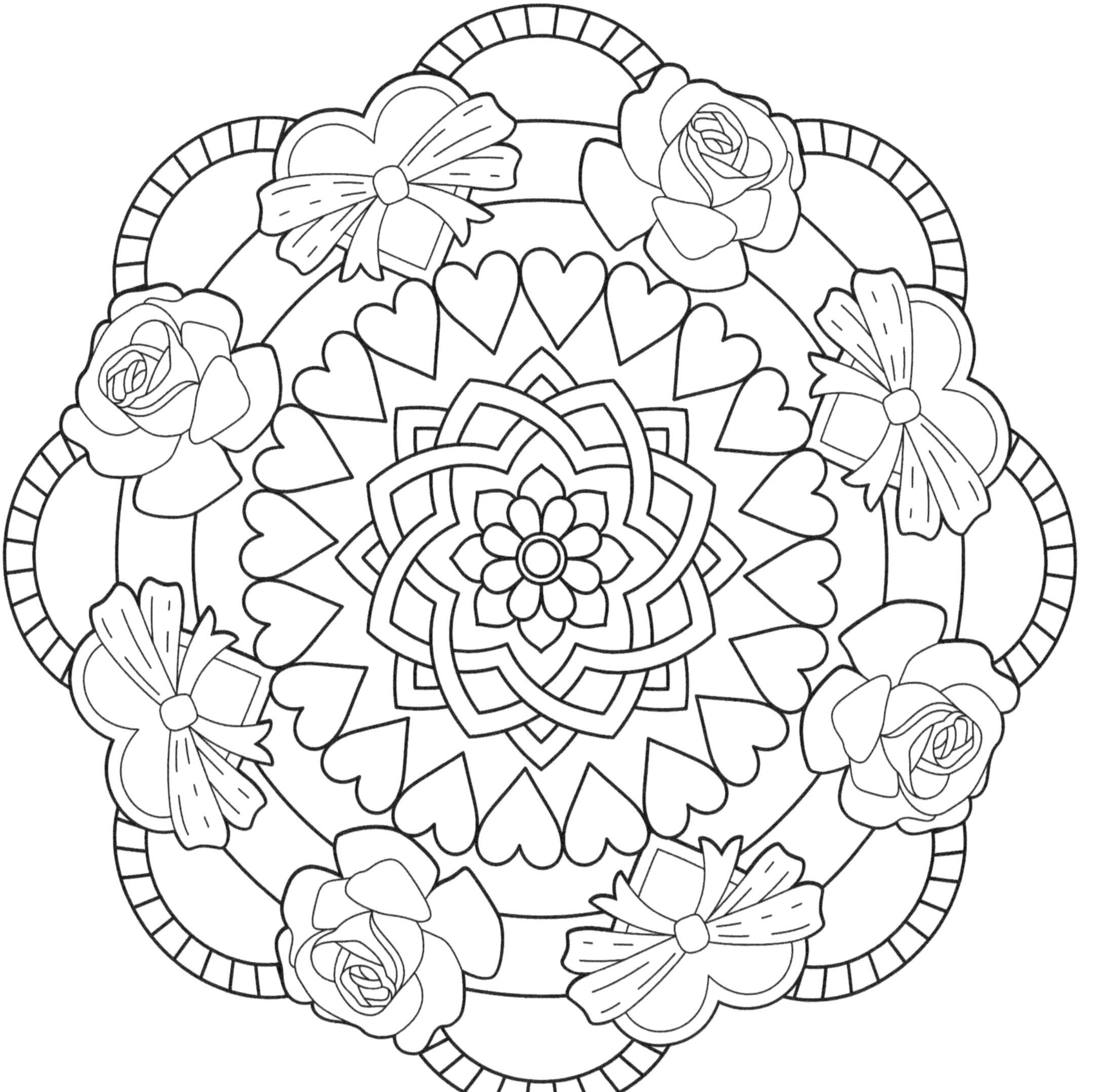

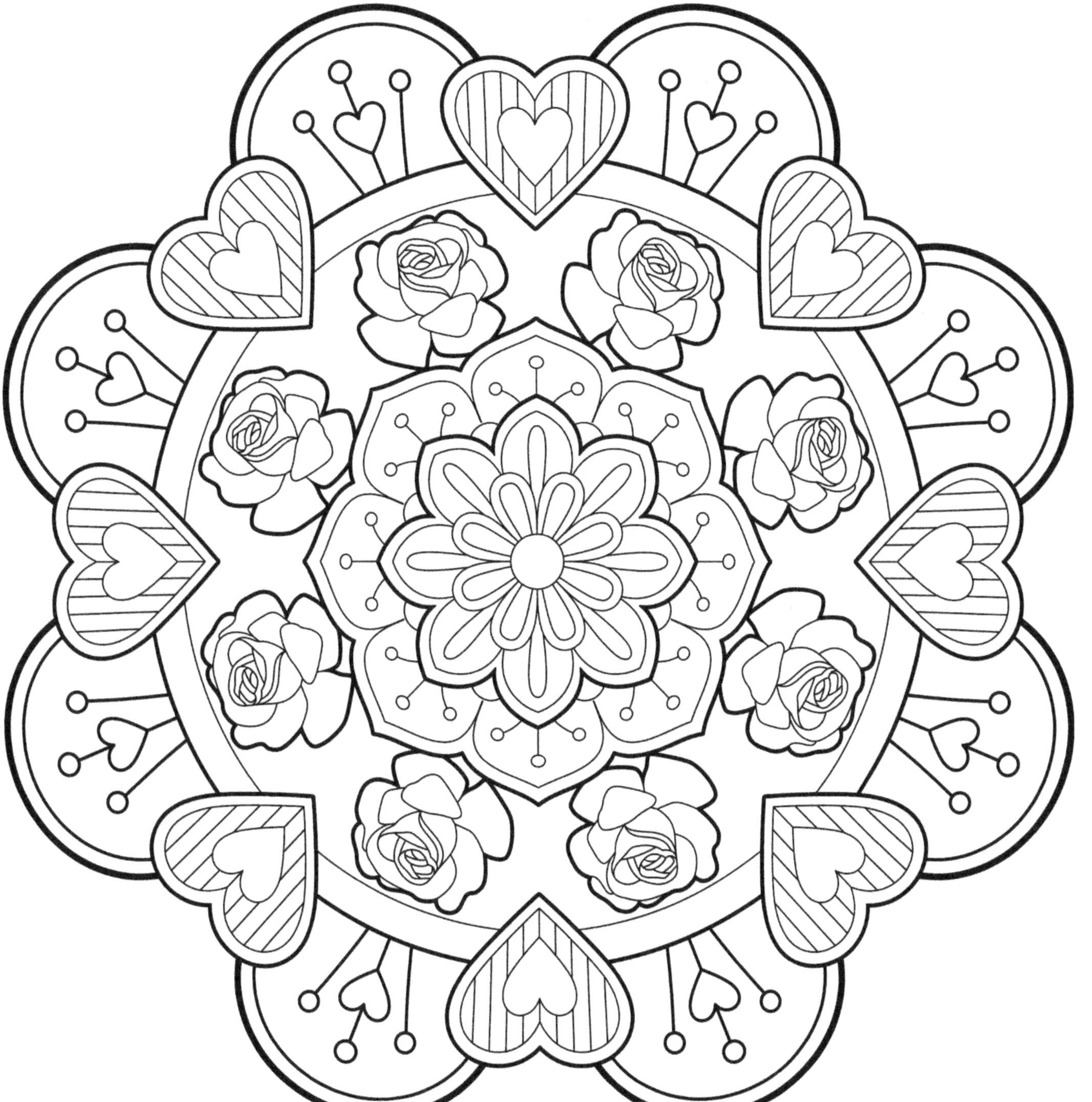

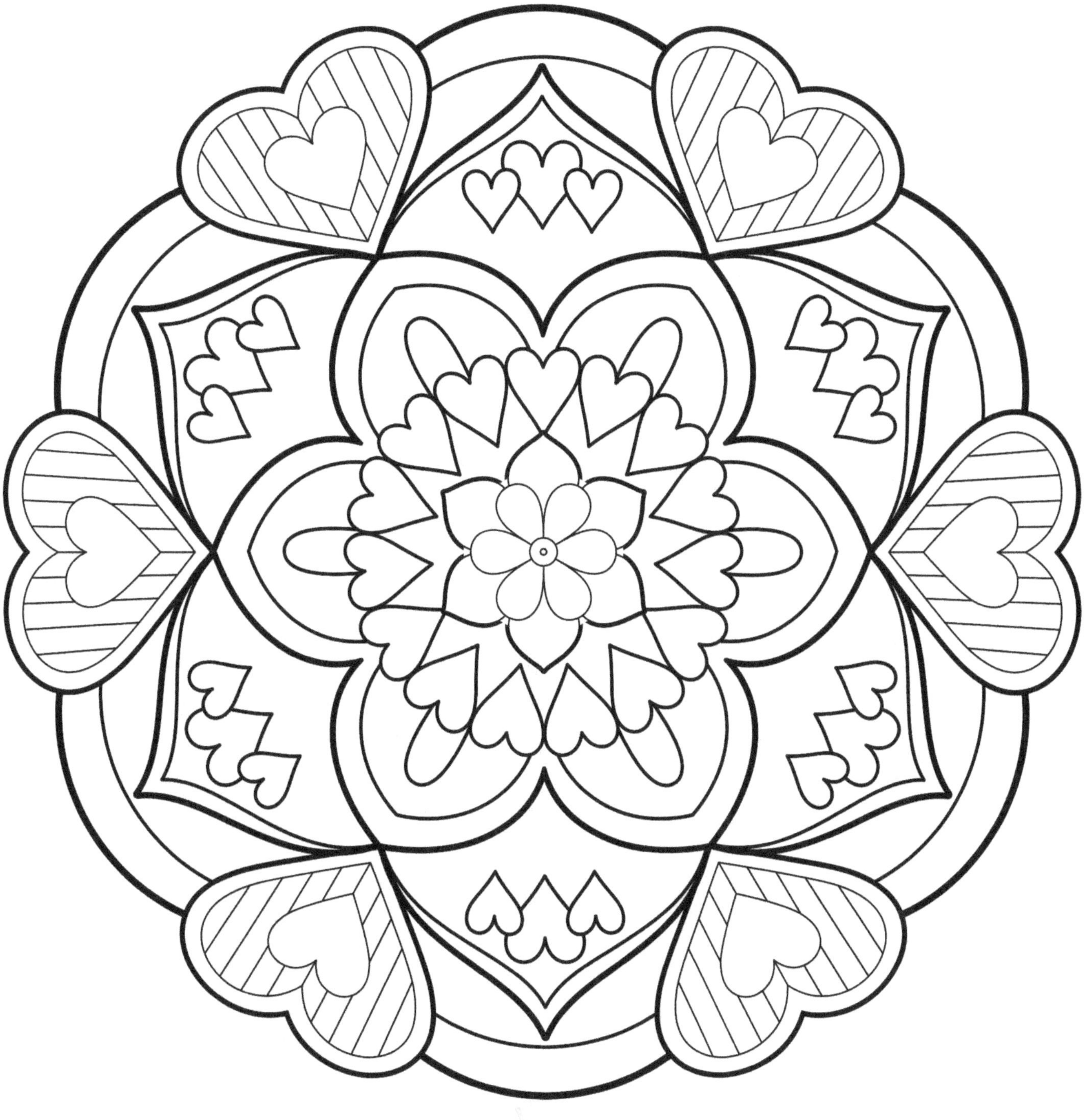

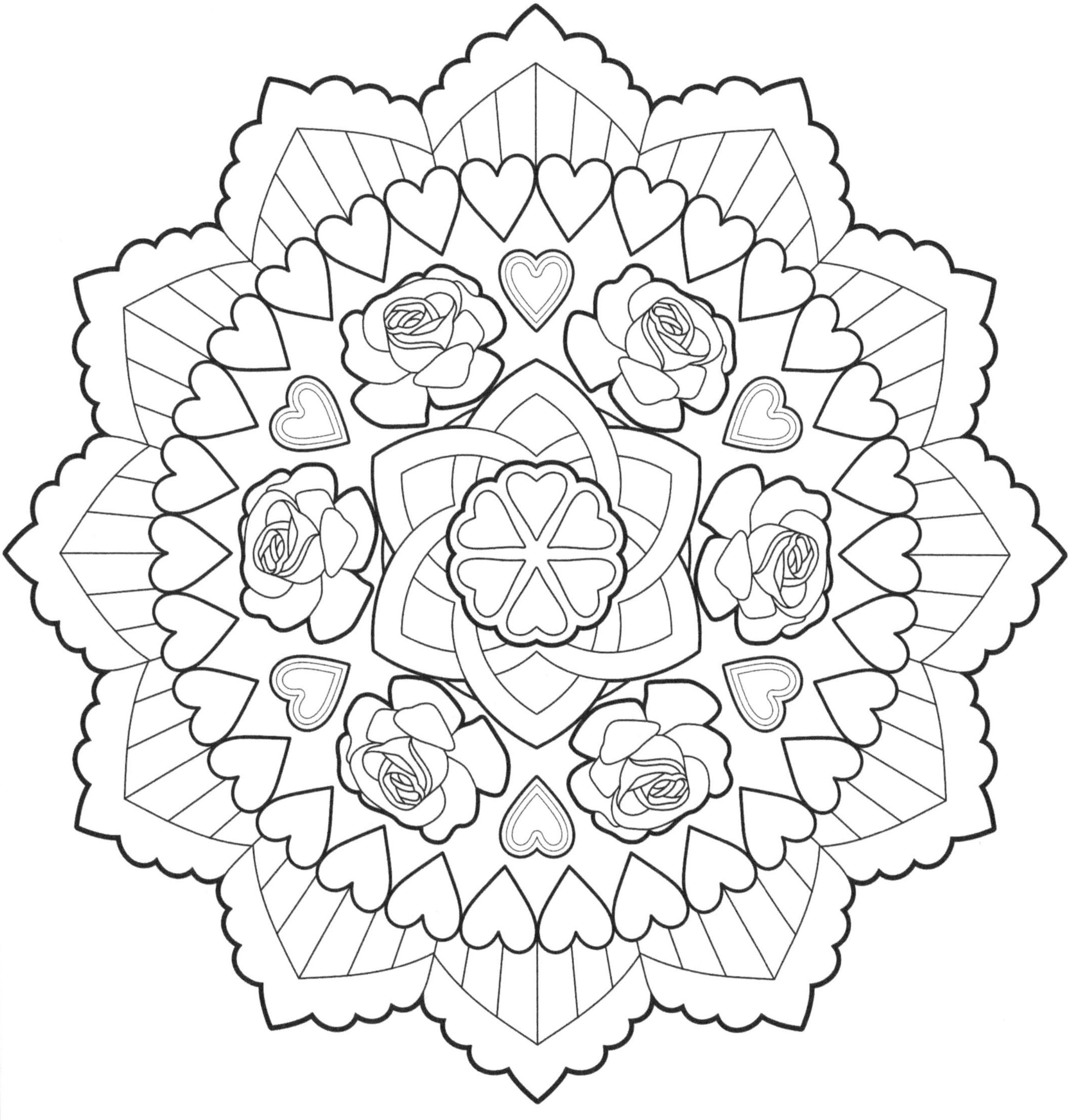

www.ingramcontent.com/pod-product-compliance
Lightning Source LLC
Chambersburg PA
CBHW080443220526
45465CB00007B/2753
9798600096615